D1045870

And I, Francis

BX
4700
.F69
D85
1986

SALZMANN LIBRARY
St. Francis Seminary
3257 South Lake Drive
St. Francis, Wis. 53235

AND I, FRANCIS

The Life of
Francis of Assisi
in Word and Image

TEXT BY

Lauren Glen Dunlap

PAINTINGS AND PRINTS BY

Kathleen Frugé-Brown

WITHDRAWN

CONTINUUM

NEW YORK · LONDON

2000
The Continuum International Publishing Group Inc
370 Lexington Avenue, New York, N.Y. 10017

The Continuum International Publishing Group Ltd
Wellington House, 125 Strand, London WC2R 0BB

Copyright © 1996 by Lauren Glen Dunlap
and Kathleen Frügé-Brown

All rights reserved. No part of this book may be
reproduced, stored in a retrieval system, or transmitted, in any
form or by any means, electronic, mechanical, photocopying,
recording, or otherwise, without the written permission
of The ContinuumPublishing Company.

Printed in the United States of America

Library of Congress Cataloging-in-Publication Data

Dunlap, Lauren Glen
    And I, Francis : the life of Francis of Assisi in word and image / text
by Lauren Glen Dunlap ; paintings and prints by Kathleen Frugé-Brown.
    ISBN 0-8264-0867-2   ISBN 0-8264-1272-6 (pbk)
    1. Francis, of Assisi, Saint, 1182-1226.   2. Christian saints—
Italy—Assisi—Biography.   3. Assisi (Italy)—Biography.
BX4700.F69D85   1996
271'.302—dc20   96-24239
                                                            CIP

Grateful acknowledgment is made to:
Paulist Press for permission to use material from "The Canticle of
Brother Sun," "A Letter to a Minister," and "The Parchment Given to
Brother Leo," reprinted from *Francis and Clare* by Regis J. Armstrong, O.F.M., CAP,
and Ignatius C. Brady, O.F.M., © 1982 by The Missionary Society of St. Paul
the Apostle in the State of New York. Used by permission of Paulist Press.

Art Resource for the photo, and permission to reprint it, of Giotto di Bondone's *The
Funeral of Saint Francis*. Bardi Chapel. S. Croce, Florence, Italy.

"A Troubadour Lyric" by Jaufré Rudel de Blaye is from *Anthology of
Troubador Lyric Poetry,* edited and translated by Alan R. Press. University
of Texas Press, Austin, 1971.

The lyric "Can l'erba fresch'e.lh folha par" by Bernard de Ventadour
is taken from the album *Troubadour Songs: Medieval Lyrics from England, France and Norway*
by Paul Hillier and Stephen Stubbs. London: Hyperion, 1984.

Photos of Kathleen Frugé-Brown's work by Ken Wagner.

for Greg
       K.F.-B.

for Gareth and Wendy
       L.G.D.

Francis Gives Alms to a Leper
linoleum block print
16" × 12"

 HIS IS HOW God breathed into me, Brother Francis, a new life. When I was in sin, it seemed too bitter to me even to look at lepers, and then God himself led me among them and taught me mercy with them. What had seemed bitter now became sweet for both soul and body. And after that I didn't wait long before leaving the world.

I said so in the testament I dictated the day before I died. And knowing that our sister, Bodily Death, embraces each of us in time, I got ready then to welcome her and spoke only briefly and yet of first things first. Indeed, meeting the leper on the road was the beginning of my new life.

When young, I loved what was lovable. My father was a rich cloth-seller and made sure I always dressed well and had money to spend. My friends were the sons of Assisi's wealthy. Not all were of noble birth but all had noble bearing and each was nobly outfitted. They looked to me and I led the way. We ate as only those with the good appetite, good teeth, and good digestion of youth may eat. We danced. We drank a lot and sang—*Chantant et jolie!*—*Singing and merry,* we sang and we were. We loved to sing the French songs of lovers in love with love and unfailingly true to the object of their love, their lady.

> I shall have no other than her
> Whom I have loved with a true heart—
> I have given her my love,
> Never shall I part from her,
> Come snow or frost—
> —*De li pour noif ne pour gelée!*

For good reason I was named Francis, the Frenchman.

I sought happiness in beauty and pleasures. I sought it in glory as well—I rode to war in a suit of armor and I returned from war and from a year in prison in Perugia, unsuited and ill. In time I could get out of bed. Back with my old friends, themselves returned from war, I again led the way. But I began to realize that I sought my happiness in wrong places. There was one supper I remember at which it suddenly seemed that the food in my belly soured and the wit around me coarsened. Nobility seemed vulgarity. My own pampered body and my companions' smooth young faces and strong limbs seemed no more than worm food. I saw that the beauty we were trying to gather around us and create for ourselves was ugliness.

I saw the same sun and moon and stars that I had seen previously, the same olive trees on the hillsides, field poppies and larkspur, the sparrows, the dragonflies, the flocks of sheep—but now, underlying and overlaying and shot through their beauty, I began to see the beauty of the One their very existence praised, the beauty of the Most Beautiful. And I began to long to know and to praise that One as they did. I began to seek beauty in the One who created my very apprehension of beauty.

Even so, I wavered. My knees would grow sore and my skin cold as I tried to pray through the night. I once went to fetch my good riding boots then remembered I had given them away. Why did I not wear my new silk shirt, my father wanted to know, and what made me grow pale, my mother asked, and was I thinner, was I ill? My supper was some scrap of something taken alone but my thoughts were of friends laughing together, their handsome faces glowing with gaiety and the good food my suppers had been famous for. I imagined a succulent roast pigeon. I imagined the smell and texture of an excellent goat cheese with fine herbs, the lusciousness of a perfectly ripe fig with cream, the first sip of that excellent wine from Jacob's vineyard. That wine—I had no doubts that it was a thing of great beauty.

An image grew fixed in my mind, of the old hunchbacked woman who lived at the edge of town. If I give up beauty, beauty will give me up, I kept thinking—I'll end up like her unless I leave off what I've begun—indeed, in some hours of the night I was uncertain what it was I had begun. For days and nights together I saw that hillock hump as big as the rest of old Anna and I saw her twisted face and her toothless mouth like a dark pit into which a person could fall and keep falling. The idea refused to leave. I was, in short, terrified.

But then God spoke to me. *If you want to know me, you must hate what your body formerly loved and wanted. Replace what you have loved by way of your senses with what must be loved by way of your spirit. Then all that formerly seemed sweet and pleasant to you will become bitter and unbearable and the things that formerly nauseated you will satisfy you with sweetness.*

Of course I promised I would. And without knowing what I would be called on to do or how then I would do it, I certainly knew this, that I no longer saw the old woman. This is how I gave my word of honor as a knight gives his word to his lady that I would take the bitter for sweet.

And I would not fail the God who exchanged sweet heaven for bitterest death on earth. I would by God's grace struggle to win against my enemy myself.

In my relief I never stopped to reflect on what sight it was that most bitterly sickened me above all sights, above a score of hunchbacked old women. And yet I didn't have long to wait. The next day I saddled Leon from among my father's horses and rode into the countryside just beyond the city. After morning rain, the sun had come out. Fragrant steam rose from the ground and puddles reflected blue sky and leaves dancing with delight. I thought, I remember, only of the smell of raindamp earth and the good leather of my horse's saddle.

Before I saw, I heard. Although I had never before heard the muffled, leaden clapper, I knew it immediately from many nightmares. You see, in my old life, I couldn't stand the sight of lepers— could never even view their dwellings from less than two miles away and then had to pinch closed my nostrils. I had given alms sometimes, but through a middleman, my face averted and my nose held. And yet here was a leper not ten yards from where I rode.

Leon stopped. My stomach turned. I thought I must vomit.

No city near Assisi would burn or bury alive its lepers as some others did, our cities only ordering by law that any leper must avoid narrow lanes, must wear shoes and gloves, must when answering a man met in the road stand downwind. I couldn't have said which way the wind blew then. I couldn't perhaps have said what my own name was. For that moment I knew nothing besides my sickness and the urge to flee.

Then I remembered. I had given my word and knew the chance to be a perfect knight was worth risking everything for.

He approached me with the gait of someone seeking to mount a stair. Round watery eyes with big veins looked up unblinking from his sagging face. The musty sodden smell of unwashed cloth, unwashed flesh, and a sharper smell of illness pricked my nostrils. His nose was mostly gone. His closed mouth stretched away far to either side of his face. Leon shuddered and whickered but stood still. The man outstretched his hand to me and I saw he wore no glove.

I grasped it then and quickly bent and kissed it. His hand remained outstretched. Remembering my wallet I took it and held it to him. He gripped my hand in one of his and with the other gripped the wallet so tightly that it deformed in his grasp before being swallowed into a sleeve. Then I recollected myself to jump to the ground to embrace him.

He gave the kiss of peace on my lips—I could not have said

where his lips were—and I remember his breath was no stench but sweeter even than the rained-on earth.

He turned and walked away and I mounted my horse, filled with amazement and joy at the great gift given me.

I had seen the face of God! I had received the kiss of Jesus Christ! This is how my true life began.

�֎

Soon I went to live with the lepers at San Lazzaro nearby, eager to be near and to serve those there. I fed and washed them, wiped and bandaged their ulcers, laundered and mended their clothing, and very often kissed them. A person's skin may need comfort in many ways.

Later I urged the brothers who were given to me to serve these who were made in the image of God and especially urged my brothers to serve these men for the sake of the love of Jesus who for our sake was considered like a man with leprosy. Our great privilege was to live with these the world had cast out and disinherited and serving them serve Jesus himself. In time so many brothers came that all of us could not live in one place, but there was in any case much to do in many places.

One day certain brothers who took care of sick persons came to me. There is a man with leprosy among us, they said, so sick and so irate that all are convinced he is possessed by an evil spirit. We have come to ask what to do.

Now these brothers would sooner have eaten dung than they would have swallowed the nonsense that claimed lepers by nature were irate—although pain often makes a person irritable—or were insanely suspicious or greedy or insatiably lustful. They no more saw a leprous body as emblem of a vice-ridden soul than they saw earth from an anthill or turtle's blood as cure for a leprous body. And yet my own eyes could see the bruises and cuts given the brothers by the man they tried to nurse.

Our worst wounds, they said, come not from this man's hands but from his mouth—foul words and sharp insults and yet worse curses against God.

In short, no one could be found now to care for the man.

We've meekly endured his insults, they said, but we're afraid to share his sin or seem to support his evil. Do you not think, they asked, that the man should be abandoned?

But a man with leprosy has no place to go and no one to take him up.

I traveled with them back to that place.

The smell hung heavy over the man huddled on his bed in a corner apart from the others. His skin all over was purplish blotches and eruptions grown encrusted and cracking and erupting again.

I knelt close enough that he would not have to move his head to see me.

God give you peace, my dear brother, I told him.

He spat out, What peace can I have from a God who's taken from me all peace and everything good and made me all rotten and stinking? His rasping voice was lost in breathlessness.

My dear son, I began, be patient because the weaknesses of the body are given to us in this world by God for the salvation of the soul. So they are worth much when borne patiently.

His face contorted. His bared teeth were like a dog's, long in gums mostly gone and giving off a bloody matter. He said, How can I bear patiently this constant pain racking me day and night? Not only am I crucified by my sickness but I am sorely wronged by these brothers of yours.

And then he said what pierced me—

Because there is not one who serves me the way he should.

Not one.

It was then that I heard the voice of God in the man's hoarse whisper and saw the face of Christ crucified, lesions on his eyes and mouth. And I remembered the psalm saying God looks down from heaven on us to see if there is any that understands and seeks God, and yet all have gone aside, it says, they are all together become filthy, there is not one that does good, no, not one. And I thought that his Not one was God's Not one.

I excused myself to pray alone and asked God to make me what I should be to the man and begged pardon for addressing the man's question and not addressing the man himself. Then I returned to the man.

Dear son, I told him, I want to take care of you since you're not satisfied with the others.

All right, he said. But what more can you do for me than the others?

I'll do whatever you want.

He blinked twice rapidly and said, I want you to wash me all over—I smell so bad I can't stand it.

Immediately I had the brothers boil water with sweet marjoram and other herbs that grew nearby. The smell of the herbs filled the place as I undressed the man, careful to listen for any quick intake of breath to tell me I hurt him. When the bath was ready, I washed him with my hands while one of the brothers poured water.

The crusts grew soft and dissolved in the water and the purple lesions grew lighter and the pale skin gained color until the water had touched every part of him and his skin was fresh as a child's.

When the man saw his skin become new he wept bitterly and asked God for the same mercy on his soul that he had received on his body.

I thanked God and hurried to leave town so that people would not hear about a miracle and come running to me. You see, I did nothing. My God simply used my hands.

Two weeks later I received word that the man had died a good death in the peace of God and I rejoiced.

A Troubadour Lyric

by Jaufré Rudel de Blaye

Quan lo rius de la fontana   When the fountain's stream
S'eclarzis, si cum far sol,   runs clear as it used to do, and
E par la flors aiglentina,   the wild rose flower appears,
E.l rossinholetz el ram   and the nightingale on the
Volf e refranh ez aplana   bough turns and softens and
Son dous chantar, e l'afina,   smoothes its sweet song, and
Be's dregz qu'ieu lo mieu refranha.   refines it, it's indeed right that
          I should soften mine.

Amors, de terra lonhdana,   Oh love, of distant land, for
Per vos totz lo cors mi dol;   you my whole heart aches; and
E no.n puesc trobar mezina   I can find no cure if not in
Si non al vostre reclam,   your alluring call, with pangs
Ab maltrait d'amor doussana   of sweet love in meadow or
Dinz vergier o part cortina,   within curtained chamber,
Ab dezirada companha.   beside the desired companion.

Pus totz jorns m'en falh aizina,
No.m meravilh si n'ai fam;
Quar anc genser Crestïana
Non fo—ni Dieus non o vol—
Juzïa ni Sarrazina.
Ben es selh paguatz de mana
Qui de s'amor ren guazanha!

Since always ease of it forsakes
me, I marvel not that I hunger
for it; for there was never
Christian lady more fair—nor
does God wish there to be—
nor Jewess nor Saracen lady.
He is indeed fed with manna
who wins anything of her love!

De dezir mos cors no fina
Vas selha ren qu'ieu pus am;
E cre que volers m'enguana
Si cobezeza la.m tol.
Que pus es ponhens d'espina
La dolors que per joi sana,
Don ja non vuelh qu'om m'en
    planha.

My heart never ends its
longing for her whom I love
most; and I fear lest my will
should cheat me if urgent
desire robs me of her. And
sharper than thorn is the pain
which by joy is healed and for
which I want no one ever to
pity me.

Francis Renounces Material Possessions
linoleum block print
16" × 12"

· 2 ·

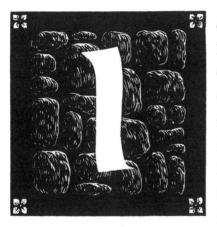 OUTRUN THE STORY, THOUGH. I had, as I said, seen the face of God, received the kiss of Jesus Christ—the kiss of the leper who met me on the road. I knew by my joy that I was changed. What I did not know was where to take that joy and what to do with it there.

Often I would go into the hills east of the city to pray. One day when I was imploring God to show me that where and what, I felt certain I would know soon. This you can imagine made me almost giddy with gladness. When I saw my old friends in town they had no notion of what was going on and said I must be in love. I am, I am! I told them.

And perhaps you are thinking of marrying? they pressed.

Ah yes! I said. Wait till you see the bride I take! A lady more beautiful and joyous, noble and rich you have never seen!

We all laughed. I believe they thought I was joking and they laughed at the joke while I laughed from sheer gladness. They didn't know I spoke of Lady Poverty.

Three days later when out walking I passed by the little church of San Damiano about half a mile outside Assisi, half buried among oak trees. Not many stopped there any more as small bits of dislodged stone sometimes fell onto their praying heads and the chinks in the walls let in not only wind but rain. I stopped inside to pray, kneeling before the image of the poor Christ suffering naked on the cross. Then I heard a voice speak my name tenderly as a lover—Francis, go and repair my house. You see it is all falling down.

I thought I had lost my senses or else soon would but then heard again the voice this time with my mind's ear and knew that only Christ himself could speak with such sweet compassion. I did then return to my senses—that is, I felt my knees and back and smelled the musty walls—and jumped up resolved to devote myself completely to repairing tumble-down little San Damiano. I hurried home making plans.

I still have to laugh when I see myself running back to town. Losing my senses should have been the least of my concerns. It was my senses that felt and heard the breeze whistling through the holes in San Damiano's walls and it was my senses that saw the pigeon feathers float down through the hole in its roof. Only much later did I realize that God had sent me to go repair the invisible church Christ wooed to be his own dear bride. But then as I ran I thought only of repairs with stone and mortar and I knew such repairs needed money.

My father was away from the shop and his two clerks looked at me closely when I came in breathless and flushed. It had been weeks since I had helped in the shop. I greeted them happily, saying I came on business of my father—meaning my father God—it was a day of *double entendre* unnoticed.

I grabbed the most expensive scarlet damasked silk and wool brocade, fit for a king's wedding clothes. I took as much as I could carry in my arms, wrapped it, and rode Leon at a gallop to Foligno. There I sold the cloth to a man I knew would recognize its value and sold Leon to one I knew would treat him kindly.

Free of all luggage, I started back, wondering what to do next.

The way was much slower on foot than it had been on Leon's back. For neither the first nor the last time walking aired out my brain and exercised my heart. By the time I reached San Damiano I had remembered the sufficiency of God and wanted to do with the money in my wallet nothing except get rid of it. I hurried to find the priest in charge there. Father Rufino was an old man I knew well enough to know he had no money and who knew me well enough to know I had always had plenty to spend on pleasant extravagances.

Sir Father, I began, I want to repair San Damiano. I have all the money needed for it, here, I said, holding out the wallet which I recall was fairly bulging. Will you please accept it then?

His mouth was partly open but he said nothing. When he stared at my clothing I supposed he might have been surprised to see me no longer dressed like a rich cloth-seller's son. And then I supposed I might have spoken too fast, so I repeated what I had said.

As he still said nothing, I thrust the wallet into his hands. The father held it a little away from himself frowning and cocking his head a bit as he stole a glance at the money inside. I heard the quick intake of his breath before he slapped the wallet shut.

No, he said, flat out, and the wallet was back in my hands.

You never before refused the money I gave San Damiano, I said.

He spoke each word as one might lay a gold coin on a counter—This, he said, is a lot of money.

But it is nothing! I said.

But your father would not agree, I suspect.

And that, I knew, was certainly true. There could be no argument there.

So I told him that I had seen God and that everything was different now—everything!

You will at least let me stay here, won't you? I was on my knees by then. I pleaded with him until probably I simply wore him out. He knew I was sincere if he knew nothing else and agreed to let me stay.

Then you will take the money as well, I asked, jumping to my feet.

Your father is a powerful man, he said, shaking his head. And this much money is too much money.

Ah! I said, laughing, but this money is nothing! Truly! And I tossed the wallet over my shoulder, twirling to see the end of its arc as it landed on a small windowsill high up at the back of the room. A spray of dust flew up around it, sparkling in the sunshine as if for joy, and I thought Yes! yes, sit there with the rest of the dust!

But there remained the matter of my father. Peter Bernardone considered money to be more than dust. Much more.

Two days later when a friend came to San Damiano to tell me that my father had found out my whereabouts and was coming with others to take me, I felt no surprise. I did though feel very much afraid. I had seen my father's anger hurl a man down stairs. I had seen it strike a man so hard it lifted him off his feet. I was new at serving Christ and so I mistook such anger as something to avoid instead of to welcome.

The friend showed me a cave nearby and in that small darkness I hid for a month. At first I implored God to save me from my pursuers and then in time, more and more, to give me the means to fulfill my desire. The tears that accompanied the latter request were thinner and cleaner than the earlier tears. I ate very little that month in part to pray with fasting and in part because the friend feared he was watched and so came only seldom. And yet I only seldom thought of him and more seldom than that thought of my body but more and more of the love that spoke my name and told me Repair my house.

One day when I cried to God to give me my desire, there in the cave I remembered myself embraced by God and felt a joy so sharp it pierced my skin and for a moment seemed to collapse my lungs and then fill them more than I had known they could be filled. I tried briefly but was no longer able to pray as I had before—the only words that made any sense at all were thanks to God and it was laughing and sighing and shaking my head that I began to scold myself for being a lazy coward and still scolding crawled out of the cave. Unused to walking upright I felt like a little child just learning first steps.

On the way to town I stopped for a drink of water and for a long moment did not recognize the face reflected in it. When I drank it was as though I both kissed and was kissed by the water and I marveled at the gift of it, like a friend and a sister, pure as God's love, supremely lowly and supremely precious.

Nor did the first person who saw me when I walked into town recognize me immediately. When I smiled at him though he said my name as if the taste of it in his mouth were new and little to his liking. He ran off and then there was no question of my going unrecognized. I caught up with the man speaking with others and they followed me as I passed by. First one and then another shouted and others joined them shouting Fool! Most yelled Crazy! Crazy! Some threw mud and others stones. Francis Bernardone! Francis Bernardone! and I hardly felt as though I recognized the name any more than at first I had recognized the face reflected in water.

A window opened and a face looked out.

You rabble! it shouted at the shouting crowd. What do you have to do with my name? What—

The eyes met mine and the voice stopped mid-shout. Face and shoulders seemed to grow bigger as though the man would jump straight down to the street. But he disappeared and in a moment was at me, his hands outstretched before his face. He threw me down and grabbed me back to my feet then threw me down again before he pulled me inside the doorway. There were more blows in the courtyard and then I was locked in a cellar closet where he visited me often.

You were to be my heir! he kept shouting. Everything I did I did for you!

On condition that I returned the money, on condition that I worked in the shop, on condition that I had no more to do with San Damiano—on and on and on with conditions—I could, he said, restore myself.

I could only say that God had restored me and that that was all I wanted.

He left me alone then.

Francis darling? came my mother's voice. Are you all right?

When I told her I was she burst into tears. Your father left town on business he put off when you disappeared. Darling you must promise me that you'll be good and do whatever your father tells you to do so that you can stay home and work in the business.

I have other business now, I told her, business I promised to do.

But darling . . . and the rest of her words escaped me. When she let me out of the cellar I thanked her and thanked God and returned quickly to San Damiano but not to the cave. I had had enough of small darkness. I walked steep paths leading through fields stretching to the plain, in high spirits and certain of God's goodness and love to me.

As I was sorting stones behind the church one day I heard the voice of my father nearby bellowing If I can't recall him to his senses I can at least drive him out of the country so I need never lay eyes on him again!

I stepped inside to greet him, very glad he had come. He rushed at me.

Let me tell you, I said, that your imprisonment and beatings can mean nothing to me. I would gladly undergo any evil for the name of the Christ who underwent all evil for me.

No now you listen to me you little bastard, he said. I'll be damned if I don't get back the money you stole from me.

Then I remembered the money.

You don't have to look far for the money, I said, pointing—it no more has legs to walk away than it has heart or voice to praise God.

He ran then to the windowsill and pulled a bench to the wall to reach it. I had to turn away from the expression on his face at seeing the money intact in the wallet.

Then fine, he said, wiping the dust from the wallet and from his hands. This is very fine then. Now all that is left is to complete our transaction. I'll have you before the city judges!

But you see, God has made me perfectly free and since I serve only God those men can have nothing to say to me.

Those men, you say! Then by God I'll have you before the bishop himself!

He took a step toward me at the same time I stepped toward him and said, Why yes, let's go before the bishop! I danced past him and he had to hurry to keep up with me on the way into town.

Bishop Guido granted us an audience in the cathedral. He heard out the story my father told then turned to me where I was kneeling.

Your father is highly incensed and greatly scandalized by your conduct. So if you want to serve God, you are right first of all to return him his money— Who knows whether all of it was gained in a perfectly honest way? God would not want you to use such money to restore his church.

And then just this, my son—trust in God completely and fear nothing, because God will provide everything you need to repair his own church.

Then Sir not just the money, I said but then was too happy to speak more. Words were too little and anyway I could not wait for them. I removed every thread every stitch of my clothes. Then I gathered them up and walked down the long aisle, the marble tiles cold on the bottoms of my feet, over the threshold and through the bright doorway, down the sun-warmed steps and out into the main square. Many people seemed to be waiting for me. I turned to see those who had been inside following close behind me and

I held out the clothes I had worn to the man God had used to bring me there. When he did not take them I kneeled and placed them at his feet. Then I rose and turned to face the crowd.

Listen! Listen! All grew quiet.

Before today I called Peter Bernardone my father. But now I am resolved to serve God and so I have returned to that man the money he was so perturbed about and even the clothes I wore which were his. Now I can truly say Our Father in heaven and not My father Peter Bernardone. God is my inheritance. God will clothe me.

Peter Bernardone picked up the garments and turning took two steps quickly, stopped, hurried, stopped again and finally hurried away.

Bishop Guido wrapped his cloak around me, muttering, I do not wholly understand this indeed I do not, as he bundled me back inside the cathedral. He gave me an old tunic that had belonged to one of his gardeners, a man who had recently died. With a piece of chalk I drew a cross on it, delighted at so apt a garment for a beggar.

More than anything just then I wanted the solitude and quietness that would let me hear God's dear voice when he spoke. I traveled on in joy and went to live with the lepers in Gubbio for a time before I remembered that I had work to do at San Damiano.

Poem by Anon.
from Thomas of Celano's
First Life of Francis

Behold now
he wrestles naked with
 his naked adversary and having
put off
 everything that is of this world
he thinks only about
 the things of God.
 He seeks now
so to despise
 his own life,
putting off
all solicitude for it,
that he might find peace in
 his harassed ways, and
that meanwhile
only
 the wall of flesh
should separate him from
 the vision of God.

Francis Cuts Clare's Hair
linoleum block print
16" × 12"

· 3 ·

 HEN I GREETED Father Rufino at San Damiano he said, I wondered when you would be back.

And I explained what I had been doing in Gubbio and that I had returned to repair the church as I had promised.

I see your joy and fervor, he said, but how will you repair the church with no money to buy stones?

Ah, Sir Father! Trust in God completely and fear nothing, because God will provide everything needed to repair his own church!

And then I hurried into town and did what I would do for many days after, walking through the streets and standing before the cathedral and in the main square loudly praising God and then finishing with my song I would begin to beg for stones and call out, Whoever gives me one stone will have one reward and two stones two rewards and for three stones a triple reward!

And some people laughed and spat and some cried and some

gave me stones that I carried back to San Damiano on my shoulders with the glad heart of a knight who has gained his freedom to do some small but wished for feat for his lady.

One day that first winter Angelo, one of my mother's other two sons, walked by the church and said loudly to his companion, Ask Francis to sell you a few cents worth of sweat! They laughed and merry I laughed with them and called out, *Je donnerai ma sueur à plus haut prix à mon Dieu!* His companion frowned, not understanding, and I realized what I had done and knowing that mirth is best shared called out again, this time, I will sell my sweat at a higher price to my God!

And then one day I noticed that the dinner given me by Father Rufino was a dish that had always especially pleased me on the days following Epiphany in the new year and I realized how far the kind father must have gone out of his way to supply me with food he could ill afford. This was not the life of the poor I wanted to choose. How often do the poor eat cakes with almonds?

I knew how to ask for stones but had not yet learned to ask for bread and so embracing the kind father and begging to be excused took an empty bowl and walked to town to knock at the first door I came to and beg for an alms. Then I begged at the next door and the next until the bowl was full of scraps of this and that. And I sat down and lifting up my eyes to heaven thanked God and lowering my eyes to the bowl felt my stomach turn. Never in my life had I seen such a mess let alone tried to eat it. I did not dare to taste a little and so with all the strength I could muster gulped it all of it down.

It seemed the best thing I had ever eaten in my life!

I praised and thanked God who never ceased to change what

was bitter into sweetness and to comfort me in so many ways. And from that day Father Rufino prepared no more food for me and instead I asked alms for the love of God the great Almsgiver who gives us all good things. To think that I had once been ashamed to do this act of the greatest nobility, dignity, and courtesy before God and even before the world! For you see, our Lord Jesus Christ, dearest Son of the living and all-powerful God, was a poor man and a transient and lived on alms. With all my heart I longed to walk in his footprints!

And after the Lord gave me brothers, no one showed me what I should do, but the Most High himself revealed to me that I should live according to the form of the Holy Gospel. And I had this written down simply and in a few words and the Lord Pope confirmed it for me. And those who came to receive life gave to the poor everything they were capable of possessing and they were content with one tunic, patched inside and out, with a cord and short trousers. And we had no desire for anything more. We clerics used to say the Office as other clerics did and the lay brothers said the Our Father and we were simple and subject to all.

One day at the little abandoned hut where the brothers and I stayed as we tended the poorest of the lepers at Rivo Torto I saw clearly that the Lord was glad to give me brothers and that it was not good if there was not room enough to lie down to sleep.

My dearest brothers and sons, I said, it seems like a good thing for us to ask for a small and poor church where the Least Brothers may say our hours and next to it a small and poor shelter of earth and wood where the brothers can sleep and go about their work.

And all the brothers—Bernard of Quintavalle, Peter Catanii, Giles, Sabatino, Morico, John of Capella, Philip the Tall, John of St. Constantia, Barbaro, Bernard the Watchful, Angelo Tancredi—agreed.

And so I asked Bishop Guido and he said, I have no church to give you, and then I asked the canons of St. Rufino and they said, We have no church to give you, and then I asked the abbot of the monastery of St. Benedict on Mount Subasio and he said, I will speak with my monks and you can come back to see me tomorrow.

Brother Francis, he said then the next day, I know you glory in the small and the poor. St. Mary of the Little Portion which you repaired from complete ruin is the smallest and poorest church that we have. I think, brother, it is the smallest and poorest that anyone could possibly have anywhere. What could be more to your liking? So see, brother, we grant your request. But there is one condition. If the Lord causes this little congregation of yours to grow, we want this place to become and to remain the chief of all your churches.

I rejoiced and thanked the kind abbot and told him we would take the greatest care to provide a good and holy family for it.

Only one more thing I will beg of you, Sir Father, for the love of God, and that is to grant me another condition. The Least Brothers can be in debt to no one and have no place that is our own and so we will pay rent to remind us that we own nothing in the world.

Just how do you suppose you will pay us, little Brother Francis? You allow none of your brothers to so much as touch money. What then shall I set as the price? Ah! I know. There is a little fish that may be caught in the Chiaggio running by there. Like your Least Brothers they are small but have a unique flavor. I have come to relish it.

And so each year the brothers carried a basket of fish to the monks and the good brother monks gave them a jar of oil as an alms for the love of God.

And so the brothers went to live there at once and for each one built a simple cell of clay and wood thatched with straw. Here we lived in the glory of our poverty and rejoiced in prayer and silence, fasts and vigils, cold, nakedness, and working with our hands. We tended the ill at Rivo Torto and helped the poor in the fields and traveled from city to city seeking who we might help and we never allowed God's best gift of time to be wasted. And we kept the whole place pure and fragrant with songs and praises to our God. And whoever came to us, friend or foe, thief or robber or rich man, we received with kindness.

And one day it was Clare who came to us to show me that where I had thought I brought San Damiano into good repair, stone by stone, and then moved on to repair St. Peter of the Thorns on the plain below it and after that tiny St. Mary of the Little Portion, it was she who six years later would lay in place the true foundation of San Damiano.

Clare herself was the firmest and most precious stone of the whole structure.

When Clare first came to us that day at the Little Portion we had just sat to dinner. Dearest mother, said Philip the Tall, there are two noblewomen asking to see you.

Invite them to our table, I said as all rose. We must offer them the very best we have. I hurried out to greet them with May the Lord give you peace!

From my old life I knew Clare as daughter of the noble house of Offreduccio di Bernardino. Her father Count Favarino was a knight as were other of her kin and for a moment I shrank to offer her and the Lady Bona hospitality. The only seat I could offer was the dirt floor of the tiny hut and the only feast the dish of turnips we had just sat to but her grace and courtesy showed her the truest of ladies as she greeted the least of brothers as if they were what in truth they were, my Knights of the Round Table, in the service of Lady Poverty.

Lady, I have heard of your acts of mercy and of your great almsgiving.

That is little, she said. That is merely out of my family's great wealth. I would give my very self. She hurried to speak more.

The fragrance of your reputation has spread through the whole of Spoleto and farther, she said. And I myself hear and see the life you have with the brothers and I have come because of it—because of the song I heard you sing—

> Therefore hold back nothing of yourselves for yourselves
> so that He who gives himself totally to you
> may receive you totally.

This is what you sang. This is what I want with my whole heart.

I have asked our God to direct my steps into the right way and have come to realize that it is much simpler than I realized. We can simply walk in our Lord's footprints. This is what you said. This is what you have shown me. As you follow the teaching and the footprints of our Lord Jesus Christ so, Brother Francis, I would follow yours.

I seek no followers, I told her. And they who would follow must count the cost. We have been called to heal wounds and to unite what has fallen apart and to bring home those who have lost their way. We speak the words of peace and all the more must have peace in our own hearts. We seek that none may be provoked to anger or scandal by us but rather may be drawn to peace and goodwill through our gentleness. We know many insults, hardships, and cold nights covered only with the blanket of Lady Poverty.

And as I spoke, Clare's face shone as if she were an angel. She seemed like Lady Poverty herself, a bride joyful and beautiful, when she said, Christ calls me to follow him. Christ calls and I will throw off all things that would burden me so that I can run after him.

And it was in that moment God revealed to me that Clare and those who would follow her in a second order must be called not Least Sisters but Ladies.

Clare left the world with the bishop's blessing and her family's curses. The night of Palm Sunday she left her family's home through the door of the dead. Unlike the others who passed there, she had not died but she was as quit of the world as if she had. The brothers sang songs of praise to our God and held lighted candles as they went to meet her and her aunt the Lady Bona coming through the woods. And yet it was Clare herself who was a clear shining light to all the Least Brothers that night and from that night forward. God truly had provided everything needed to repair his own church.

Clare knelt before the altar of St. Mary of the Little Portion renouncing the world and vowing to live with nothing of her own and in chastity and in obedience and in doing so to embrace and be embraced by the poor crucified One.

You have chosen holy poverty as your delight and your spiritual and bodily treasure, I said. Guard her well and let no one take her from you.

Beneath her cloak Clare wore a rough tunic and no shoes. Brother Leo had borrowed shears for the task at hand and brothers Bernard of Quintavalle and Peter Catanii brought their candles near that I might see to help Clare exchange her long hair for the tonsure of a religious. Her hair gleamed gold in the candlelight and seemed like the richest of crowns cast down at the feet of Christ but it was as she rose shorn that her light broke out like the dawn.

And indeed the dawn was breaking as I led the Lady Clare to the Benedictine nuns of St. Paul at Bastia. And it was about two hours past dawn and not yet time to recite the hours when I returned but when I came into the Little Portion there were the brothers standing in a circle before the altar with their heads bowed. I came near and saw that they were gathered around the golden pool of hair that lay where it had fallen.

And so, my sons, has no one swept the floor?

Ah father, said Giles, this beautiful stuff seems to belong more to heaven than earth. Brother John came to sweep the church and could not bear to treat it as if it were rubbish.

No of course not, I said. Let us give it as an alms to our sisters the birds for them to make their nests more strong and beautiful.

And I knelt and gathered the soft gold in my hands and the brothers each helped gather the rest and followed me outside where we laid it about on the acacia hedges.

Our Sister Lark who wears a hood like a religious, said Brother

Barbaro, will be especially pleased. But it turned out to be Sister Crow and Sister Jackdaw who best employed the alms given them by the Lady Clare.

When her uncle knights came to take the Lady back they failed to show the gentle courtesy that befits a true knight. They cursed and flattered and promised then cursed again the Lady Clare who stood unmovable where she had laid hold of the altar cloths until her uncle Monaldus stepped forward and putting his foot on the altar step said, Enough is enough, my girl, you'll come back with us this minute.

I cannot be moved, the true Lady told him.

You'll come back with us this minute or by God's wounds I'll snatch you bald!

And at that the Lady Clare bared her tonsured head and then the shouting stopped and Clare's voice rang out to say again she would not be moved from serving the God she loved. Soon they left her alone and the next day she removed to San Angelo di Panzo, a Benedictine nunnery on the side of Mount Subasio. And there she stayed until we made San Damiano ready for her and the other ladies by building cells near the chapel like the cells we brothers lived in at the Little Portion, of clay and wood, where the ladies could live as the brothers lived, in constant prayer and in working with their hands, caring for one another and tending the sick.

And by then the Lady Clare's sister Agnes had joined her. And they were joined in time by her younger sister Beatrice and her mother Ortolana, her nieces Amata and Balvina, and her childhood friends Pacifica, Benvenuta, Philippa, Cecelia, and Christina and then by others.

The Ladies Clare and Agnes moved to the place prepared for

their rest and work and joy in the last week of April when the pomegranates and lilac were in bloom against the gray stone walls. For the Lady Clare, with gayest solemnity and most solemn gaiety stepping inside those walls, here was perfect freedom.

Francis's Form of Life for Clare

Because it was God who inspired you to make yourselves daughters and servants of the most high supreme King and heavenly Father, and to take the Holy Spirit as your spouse by choosing to live according to the perfection of the Holy Gospel, I resolve and promise you for myself and for my brothers that I will always have that same loving care and special solicitude for you as for them.

Francis Builds a Snow Family by Moonlight
linoleum block print
16" × 12"

· 4 ·

ND MORE BROTHERS CAME. They gave up all that they owned, renounced themselves, took up their cross, and naked followed the naked Christ. And having left the world we had nothing else to do except to follow the will of our dearest Lord and to please him. With great joy we rejoiced among us and were comforted by our faithful lady, Poverty. And more came to rejoice with us and to be comforted. And we resolved to hold fast to poverty everywhere just as we did at the Little Portion. My Least Brothers went out, to Lombardy, Tuscany, Apulia, and Sicily and to Spain and to France and even to the land where our Lord Jesus walked. The Sultan Malik-al-Kamil treated Brother Illuminato and me with great kindness.

And each May as Pentecost approached, all the Least Brothers came back together at St. Mary of the Little Portion and we rejoiced together and spoke of how we could practice poverty more perfectly.

As there were many brothers, there were many temptations. Some brothers would have forsaken poverty. They imagined that they were living more sensibly in that way. Sensibly? Miserably! It is a great misery and a miserable weakness, I wrote to all the brothers, that when you have Christ present with you in this way, you concern yourselves with anything else in the entire world.

One day when I had come to the hermitage of St. Eleutherius, not far from Contigliano, in the neighborhood of Rieti, where a young brother was living, the brother came to ask me to consent to his owning a psalter.

My son, I told him, the Emperor Charles, Roland, and Oliver, knights who were valiant in battle, spared no hardship and no labor to gain a great victory. Others were content to sing about their deeds. Our concern is not to read about great adventures and holy deeds but to do them.

And after that the young Least Brother came to me again and told me he was still eager to have the psalter. Let us be eager, I told him, to pray and let us be eager to ask alms and to work with our hands and to have nothing to do with ownership so that we may truly and fully possess all things in God.

And then again the next night the young brother came to me as I sat near the fire to warm myself and he spoke of the psalter and the psalter and the psalter and the fire's kind gift of warmth left my hands and feet as I said, And when you have a psalter you will want a breviary and when you have a breviary you will install yourself in a chair like a great prelate and you will order your brother, Bring me my breviary!

And the sorrow I felt was so heavy that I reached and took a handful of ashes from the fire and put them on my head and rubbed them on myself and said That's the breviary!

I looked at his face and hurried to tell him, For you see I also was tempted to have books. But a Least Brother must be content to own nothing but a tunic and cord and drawers and, but only if need be, shoes.

I told him as I told others who asked me, Knowledge is a good thing but only as good as the actions it produces. The best sermon is a good life.

In the year that 5,000 brothers gathered at the yearly chapter something happened to astonish me greatly. I had just returned from a journey. And I entered the great forest surrounding the Little Portion and rejoiced to be returning even as a tired little bird returns to its nest. The larks sang to praise their Creator and to welcome me to that dearest of all places on earth. Stepping from the trees I was not surprised to see that the brothers to prepare for the coming of many had put up many more cells, poor little huts like the ones of the Little Portion, made of branches and mud and covered with straw and with them many more made of rush mats. Those who traveled here were guests and those who lived here were guests as well. For the sake of Jesus his dearest Lord and for the sake of Poverty his dearest lady, a Least Brother is always and in every place a pilgrim and a stranger.

I could not understand then when I saw near the huts a house made of stones cemented together and roofed with tiles. I hurried to find a brother who could explain to me this insult to Lady Poverty. And Brother Lucidas ran to meet me and embraced me and in tears told me, The people of Assisi banded together and in a few days with much haste and fervor they put up this house for the chapter that is to begin.

And will they take down this house when the chapter has ended? I asked and Brother Lucidas only shook his head.

Do not weep, dear son. If they will not take it down then we will take it down. Can you find me a ladder?

Brother Lucidas ran to get a ladder and bring with him other brothers and I came near to the house and looking at it seemed to see my sons and brothers in a time to come greatly multiplied and having lost the path on which they ran after the footprints of Jesus. And they were fallen and crushed beneath the weight of many stones and many big houses. And I seemed to hear the voice of Lady Poverty in sorrow say, You pledged me your troth and you have left me.

I will hold you and I will not let you go, I said and I heard at my shoulder, What is it you say, father?

Never mind, son. You found a ladder?

Brothers Lucidas and Juniper set the ladder against the wall and I climbed to the roof. I had climbed no ladder since repairing the roof of St. Mary's and my hands were no longer as strong as they had been then but I began to tear off the slates and tiles and soon called for the brothers to climb up with me to help.

In a little while I heard someone calling Brother! Brother! from below and looked to see a group of Assisans who had gathered. A knight among them called up Brother! What are you doing?

I am demolishing this house, I said.

But this house was built for your brothers.

My brothers should be firmly convinced that nothing belongs to us except our sins.

Brother, this house belongs to the commune of Assisi and we are here to represent the commune.

It does not belong to the brothers?

No. That is why we are telling you not to destroy this house.

Well, if this house belongs to you, I do not want to touch it, I said and I came down immediately.

It was at that same chapter that many of the brothers began to question our rule and to speak of other rules and to persuade the Least Brothers to follow other lives. And the Cardinal of Ostia, our protector the Lord Hugo, was at the chapter and listened to those who wanted to forsake Lady Poverty.

I stood and took the cardinal by the hand before all there on that day and called out to them My brothers! My brothers!

God has called me to walk in the way of humility and has showed me the way of simplicity and has in truth revealed this way for me and for all who are willing to follow me. So I do not want you to quote any other rule to me, of St. Benedict or St. Augustine or St. Bernard, or to recommend any other way or form of life except this way that God had revealed and given to me, little Brother Francis. The Lord told me that he wanted me to be a new kind of fool in this world and our Lord wants us to live by no other wisdom but this foolishness.

All were silent and the Lord Hugo said nothing. And I knew that I could only follow where God led me.

And do not mistake me. I was, I think, tempted more than any other brother. In fact I am quite sure that if the Lord had granted to the worst scoundrel as many good gifts as he had granted me, they would have been more faithful to Him than I. Truly, of the Least Brothers I was the least.

But our God loves us with tender mercy and gives us brothers and sisters to teach us faithfulness. Sister Wind helped me one winter day as I walked along the road to Celano. In her great hurry Sister Wind bit me all over and my heart began to sink and I desired to possess more than just a tunic with a cord and drawers and my heart sank even further to see that I desired to forsake my vow. And so I prayed for the grace to summon my faithfulness and climbing a hill nearby took off all my clothes and turned to face Sister Wind and joined my voice with hers in praise of our Creator. How well it would be for you, I told myself then, if you had even one tunic.

Many people when they sin or receive some other injury often blame the Enemy or some neighbor. But how can that be right when we all have the real enemy in our own power, namely, the body through which I sin. So blessed is that servant knight who, having such an enemy in his power, will always hold him captive and wisely guard himself against him because as long as he does this, no other enemy seen or unseen will be able to harm him.

And yet some of the Least Brothers were too harsh and would have wounded themselves by too long vigils and too long fasts and hurtful practices. So I told my dearest sons always and everywhere that each brother must take into account his own constitution and give his body what it needs so that it has strength to serve the spirit. Our God desires mercy and not sacrifice.

And yet stubborn Brother Ass needed hard lessons many times.

During one winter when I stayed at the hermitage of the brothers at Sartiano, our Sister Snow was kind enough to help me in the time of my greatest temptation.

For you see—I longed with such great desire to have children.

Our gracious and loving God had set me as mother over the Least Brothers and I cherished each one like an only child. And yet I could not tame my mind as it set before me pictures of children—not so many, I told myself in the worst of those bad hours—just two sons perhaps and perhaps two daughters—and my heart rushed headlong to embrace those pictures even as I longed to embrace my own darlings.

With what longing I thought of how I would hold my babes in my arms and sing them to sleep. And as they grew older I would hold their hands as they walked out in the grassy meadows among the white heath and the golden bloom. And I would watch by their beds as they slept. And as they grew older still, I would watch their limbs grow strong and hear their happy voices and teach them the names of hawthorn dogroses bullfinches nightingales dragonflies and teach them the sweet tunes my mother taught me. And my own dear children—

My own!

My!

Mine!

The words lodged like poisoned thorns beneath my skin and I wept to God to pluck them out. The picture of my sons and my daughters was a wild wind that fanned my desire until I felt the flames would consume me and leave nothing but a worthless handful of bitter ash.

How astonished I was and how appalled when people praised me. Some even called me a saint! But I knew too well that my end was uncertain and I begged them not to praise me, saying, I may yet bear sons and daughters! And so it was that I felt an awful dread to be near any woman.

This most miserable time of trial went on for a year and then another year and I often had to withdraw from my brothers because I had in me no fresh joy. Often I walked out to the forest surrounding St. Mary's to pray and weep.

I had come to Sartiano and for a time felt refreshed there where it was steep and wild like the mountains around it with no flowers or tender growing things. And perhaps that is why when the terrible longing returned it roared in upon me one night with a fierceness that shook my body and mind and soul.

And desperate like a lover who sees his lady traveling away and nearly out of sight, urgent not to be separated for a single hour from my sweetest Lord, I threw open the door to the cell where I stayed and ran naked through the snow into the garden and threw myself into a tall drift. Sister Moon watched as Brother Ass and I rolled and rolled and I rubbed him all over with snow to prevail upon him to let my heart unthaw.

I went back into the cell and put on my tunic to try to pray but the Spirit of God led me back outside to learn from Sister Snow.

And filling both my hands with snow I packed and molded it into seven forms and then standing before them I began to address this self of mine, saying, Here, look now, this big one is your wife and those next four are your two sons and your two daughters and the two last are your manservant and your maidservant because you will need them to serve you and now hurry, hurry, Francis, and clothe them all for they are dying of cold, they are blue with cold. And they must be fed. And the children must be taught to earn their living. And they must have found for them husbands and wives. And there will be no time to travel to where the Lord wants you to go and proclaim his love and great kindness.

And there will be no time to pray and seek the face of your God as you gaze at the faces of your children and they take the place of these other little ones, the spiritual children already given you. And and and—

And what?

Oh?

Oh?

Then does the thought of caring for them in so many ways trouble you? Then Francis you must take care to serve God alone.

And back inside the hut the tears that had frozen on my face warmed and ran off and then almighty God gave me the sweet gift of peace and I slept.

Francis's Letter to a Minister
[an excerpt]

And by this I wish to know if you love the Lord God and me, his servant and yours—if you have acted in this manner—that is, there should not be any brother in the world who has sinned, however much he may have possibly sinned, who, after he has looked into your eyes, would go away without having received your mercy, if he is looking for mercy. And if he were not to seek mercy, you should ask him if he wants mercy. And if he should sin thereafter a thousand times before your very eyes, love him more than me so that you may draw him back to the Lord. Always be merciful to such as these. . . .

Francis Receives the Stigmata
linoleum block print
16" × 12"

· 5 ·

UR SWEETEST LORD gave me a great many sweet gifts and sweetly saved the best till near the last, when I had come to desire it more deeply than I desired anything else. It was not as I imagined it would look or could have imagined and so it appeared to me the more unspeakably dear for that.

That gift was given to me on Mount Alverna and that dear mountain itself was a gift given by Count Orlando of Chiusi in Casentino. And this is how Alverna was given.

One time when Brother Leo and I had left the Valley of Spoleto to go to the province of Romagna, we passed by the foot of the walled city of Montefeltro with its strong castle set high on the cliff. There seemed to be much coming and going and many banners shimmering and snapping and finally a man from the village told us, A great banquet and festival are being held to celebrate the knighting of Count Brancacci. Many great noblemen, he said, have gathered here from many districts. Many singers and players have gathered also and there is a troubadour who has lately arrived from Provence. And I, he said, must take them cheeses to whet their noble appetites and tune their stomachs to their songs.

The man raised his basket to his shoulder again and hurried up the steep road.

Brother Leo, I said, I am glad we are here.

We went to the square where many of the nobles were assembled and I climbed onto a low wall in order to speak of the great goodness of God. And afterward the noblemen returned to the castle but one man drew near and said, I have heard much of you, Brother Francis, and now I myself have heard you. I would like to speak to you about the salvation of my soul.

I am glad, I said. But this morning go and honor your friends since they invited you to the festival and have dinner with them and after dinner we will talk together as much as you like.

And he went and came again and we spoke together. Brother Francis, I have a mountain in Tuscany which is very solitary and wild and perfectly suited for someone who wants to devote himself to contemplation. If that mountain would please you and your companions I would gladly give it to you for the love of God.

I thanked and praised God who knows the desires of our hearts and cares for his smallest lambs and I thanked Count Orlando for his alms. We agreed that I would send two brothers to him so that he could show them the mountain so suited for prayer and penance. And then as Leo and I turned to resume our journey, God showed that he knew yet another desire of my heart when Count Orlando called after us and asked that we join him to hear the troubadour perform his songs that evening.

The floor of the chamber we visited in the castle was strewn with violets and with red pink and white cyclamen and the air was full of music. Count Orlando led us to a chimney corner where we sat to listen to fiddles and harps and flutes and finally the songs of the troubadour. His name was Bernart de Ventadorn. One of his songs pressed its words and tune deep in my soul and when Leo and I continued on our journey, cornfields and vineyards and birds and angels more than once heard me sing

Can vei la lauzeta mover
When I see the lark beating its wings

De joi sas alas contra.l rai,
with joy against the ray of the sun,

Que s'oblid'e.s laissa chazar
until oblivious it swoons and drops

Per la doussor c'al cor li vai,
for the sweetness that enters its heart,

Ai tan grans eveya m'en ve
ah, such envy I feel

De cui qu'eu veya jauzion,
for those who enjoy love

Meravilhas ai car desse
that I marvel that my heart

Lo cor de dezirer no.m fon.
doesn't immediately melt with desire.

Ai las tan cuidava saber
Alas, I thought to know so much of love,

D'amor, e tan petit en sai.
and I know so little.

Car eu d'amar no.m posc tener
For I cannot help loving her

Celeis don ja pro non aurai.
from whom good will never be given.

Tout m'a mo cor e tout m'a me,
She has taken my heart,

E se mezeis e tot lo mon,
my self and herself and the world,

E can se.m tolc no.m laisset re
and when she left, only desire

Mas dezirer e cor volon.
and a longing heart remained to me.

That journey ended, Leo and I returned to St. Mary's and from there I sent Brother Masseo of Marignano and Brother Angelo Tancredi to Count Orlando. Angelo was himself a nobleman of Rieti before becoming a Least Brother and I relied on his courtesy and kindness. Masseo was marked by a gracious look and by natural good sense but not, I fear, a good sense of direction and no more was Angelo. I had forgotten until they returned to us at the Little Portion and told the story of how they had become lost.

When we finally arrived at the castle of Chiusi, Count Orlando welcomed us with joy and kindness, said Masseo, and insisted that we rest and sup before climbing the mountain. Fifty armed men went with us—

Fifty! I said. What for, brothers?

Masseo and Angelo looked at one another and shrugged. Perhaps to honor the order, said Masseo. Or to protect us from wild animals. Or, said Angelo, to have the pleasure of visiting such a strange and beautiful place.

It was good they were there, Masseo told, because they used their swords to cut down branches for us to build a little place when we found a spot with level ground.

But brothers, tell me if you think it is as solitary and as truly suited for contemplation as I have hoped.

They looked at one another and again at me and shook their heads and told me, Dear mother, it could not possibly be more so.

And so those two and Brother Leo and I set out. It was early August and I hoped to celebrate the feast of St. Michael with a fast of forty days before it for surely it is a gift to us to be able to honor so great a prince as Michael by offering to God some praise or special gift. I had long since given up having charge of the Least Brothers because of my body's infirmities and now had no other duty to the brothers but to pray for them and be a good example to them.

As we drew near Alverna, I stopped to rest beneath an oak along the path and began to study the landscape around me. The mountain rose above the cornfields and vineyards, dark and jagged. At its top, pine trees grew dark and straight and close together, and below the forest were steep cliffs of bare rock and huge boulders and deep crevasses, and below that the beech and oak woods where I sat suddenly aware of a great number of all kinds of birds that had come near. They flew to me. And singing and twittering and fluttering their wings they settled on my head and shoulders, in my lap and all around my feet.

Thank you for your joy and your welcome, my dears. Yes, yes. We will stay a while on this mountain.

And I rose to journey on to the hut of tree branches.

On the next day Count Orlando came with his men. I welcomed and thanked him and he begged me to ask for anything we might need. And I asked him to have a poor little cell made for me at the foot of a very beautiful beech tree that stood about a stone's throw from the brothers' place. And he did and he asked us to ask him for more and when we would not he drew us aside and said, My dear brothers, I do not want you to lack anything which you may need on this wild mountain. So I want you—and I say this once for all—just to send to my house for anything you need. And if you do not do so I will really be offended.

But when he had returned to his castle I asked the brothers to sit and told them, Now listen, my dears, don't pay so much attention to the charitable offer of Count Orlando that you in any way offend our Lady Poverty. God has called us to be Least Brothers for the salvation of the world. And God has made this contract between us and the world—that we give the world a good example and that the world provide us with what we need. So let us persevere in holy poverty.

And after that, because I could see that I was drawing near to death and still had so very much still to do and to become, I explained that I would stay alone to recollect myself with God. And I asked Brother Leo to bring me a little bread and a little water whenever it seemed right to him. And on no account, I told them, let any persons come to me but deal with them yourselves. I blessed them and went to the place beneath the beech.

One day near the Feast of the Assumption Brother Leo came to me and I asked him to go stand in the doorway of the brothers' hut and come when he heard me call. He went and I called and he came and I said, Son, let's look for a more remote place where you can't hear me when I call.

We looked and found on the south side of the mountain a place as wholly alone as any place could be, surrounded by towering rock on all sides except where we stood and on that side separated from us by a very deep chasm in the rock.

I turned and embraced Brother Leo. This is the very spot, little Brother Lamb.

But father, he said.

His forehead puckered as it did when Leo was about to cry.

But father—

Son?

This horrible chasm terrifies me. How can you cross it?

Oh that. That should be no problem, I told him. His forehead remained puckered. I don't know how I can cross it but let me think.

It took us great effort but we put a log across and walked over the log. Brother Leo was able to come when I held him by the hand and together on the other side we made a hut.

We walked together back to the other side. You must leave me now, sweet Brother Lamb. I daubed the sweat and tears from his face with my sleeve and finally pushed him toward the brothers' place.

In that place I fasted for the forty days and nights. For all that time a falcon who had a nest nearby would wake me every night before matins by singing and beating his wings against the place until I got up and said the hour. This happened each night without fail unless I was too tired or ill and then this friend would wait till later. Brother Falcon's thoughtfulness helped drive away my laziness and stimulate me to pray. And sometimes the good brother kept me company during the day.

Toward the end of the forty days Brother Ass was so weakened that I tried to comfort him with some especially delicious spiritual food and so began to think of the limitless joy to be in God's presence and then began to pray that God would grant me the grace of tasting just a little of that joy. And while my heart pondered that, all of a sudden an angel appeared in very bright light, holding a fiddle in his left hand and a bow in his right. I stared. The angel lifted the bow and drew it once upward across the fiddle and immediately that single note flooded me with all the sounds of creation mixed and melded together and yet without being con-fused—all creation's sounds were overshadowed and yet born up by that single note. Its beauty was unbearable. My senses all melted and I knew that if the angel drew the bow down again the sound would draw my soul out of my body forever. But the angel disap-peared and I was back in exile with Brother Ass and my longing.

After matins on the Feast of the Holy Cross I stood at the open-ing of the hut and prayed. And overcome with desire, I asked to be united to my dearest God to know the love which made our Lord Jesus Christ stretch out his arms on the hard wood of the cross that he might draw us into his arms' embrace. Unspeakable love. Unspeakable pain.

The dawn was still a long way off when, standing with my heart and eyes lifted up, I saw light coming down from heaven. As it came closer I could see a creature with wings of fire. As he came closer and closer I could see his hands extended and his feet joined together and fixed to a cross. Two of his wings were raised above his head and two spread out to fly and two wrapped around his body and so I knew the one I saw to be a seraph and yet what I saw was a crucified man. No—and I knew even at the time that an immortal angel could never be nailed to suffer to a cross and yet he was man and so too he was angel and so I stood amazed and also very much afraid and at the same time filled with great grief at his suffering and with very great joy to see how lovingly he looked on me. I could not understand. And I felt my heart about to break to be beheld so dear. With no words my heart called out to this one to come to me and I held up my hands to draw him closer or rather to climb nearer to him and also to hold him back. I wanted to hide, I wanted to fly to meet him, and as he approached still nearer the light grew so bright it lit up the sky like midsummer noon and lit my flesh like leaves and the light ravished my sight and became dark.

Still, you see, I have no words. Surely earth herself has no words to describe this light that pierced and filled and dissolved me, so hot it was cold, throwing open every door and crumbling every wall and in that eternal moment ah my God at last at last in that glimpse I could truly see the One who truly is and there was nothing separating me from the infinite One who loved me infinitely. And—

And then the vision disappeared.

I was back on that ledge on Alverna sometime before dawn. Around me I saw the darker darkness of the rock face and heard the wind in the trees' leaves and felt the hard earth beneath my feet. All was as it had been. Yet all was changed. The vision of the flaming light planted that light within me. And from that day to the day of my death I enjoyed the unspeakable joy of knowing and of knowing myself known by the beloved Lover. It was as if my heart had before been made of dark rock like the cliffs and now had become soft flesh. And ah my God that heart of flesh felt pain, a comforting pain inseparable from the One offering it and offering himself to his God as a holocaust. This fulfilled my deepest desire and yet the desire burned only fiercer for that.

And I was not the only one to receive a gift, for God kindly gave gifts to Brother Ass as well. I could see the sun begin to rise now above the horizon from where I stood facing east on the mountain. And as the air grew lighter I began to be able to see shapes then colors and glancing down I could see marks as of nails beginning to appear in my hands and feet just as I had seen them a little before in the crucified one above me.

And I no longer spoke to Brother Ass as to a bad-tempered and lazy beast of burden that wants to eat but refuses to work, complaining all the while.

Brother Body and I need your help, I told Brother Leo when he came at the end of the forty days. It was Brother Leo, a good friend and servant of God and simpler and purer and dearer to me than all the rest, who bandaged my hands and feet and side where the blood would not stop. And it was with Brother Leo that I set out for Assisi across the mountains to Borgo, riding an ass's colt. I grieved to ride rather than walk—but Brother Body could not walk. And I grieved to bid the dear holy mountain farewell knowing I would never again return.

I wept as we started down the mountainside even as I rejoiced to be returning to the best of places. From then until death I stayed most of the time at the Little Portion and the brothers made me welcome. And Leo stayed by me.

The Parchment Given to Brother Leo on Mount Alverna

The Praises of God
[in Francis's writing]

You are holy, Lord, the only God, You do wonders.

You are strong, You are great, You are the most high,
You are the almighty King.
You, holy Father, the King of heaven and earth.

You are Three and One, Lord God of gods,
You are good, all good, the highest good,
Lord, God, living and true.

You are love,
You are wisdom, You are humility, You are patience,
You are rest,
You are peace, You are joy,

You are justice, You are moderation, You are all our riches,
You are enough for us.

You are beauty, You are gentleness,
You are the protector,
You are our guardian and defender,
You are strength, You are refreshment,

You are our hope, You are our faith, You are our charity,
You are our sweetness,
You are our eternal life—
Great and wonderful Lord,
God almighty, merciful Savior.

The Blessing for Brother Leo
[on the back of the parchment—
dictated to Leo then signed]

The Lord bless you and keep you.
May the Lord show his face to you and be merciful to you.
May the Lord turn his countenance to you and give you peace.

May the Lord bless you, Brother Leo.

The Death of Francis (After Giotto)
linoleum block print
16" × 12"

· 6 ·

FTEN I WOULD SAY, Let us begin, brothers, to serve the Lord God for up to now we have made little if any progress. I hoped always to make a new beginning. Now at the end of my life I wanted to go back again to serving lepers as I had at the beginning when all held me in contempt and none was so cruel as to call me saint. So many visitors came to see me and I wanted to be in some remote place where no persons no cares no clamorings in my ears or in my heart would separate me from my God but only—that *only!*—this wall of flesh that I could not yet leap over.

But God in great kindness dismantled that wall stone by stone until the day it was taken down to the ground and I finally was set free to enter the kingdom of our heavenly Father.

But for those two years, Brother Body lingered unable to walk and so forced me to ride wherever I would go to visit lepers until finally Brother Body could no longer even ride and had to be carried. That was when I was staying in Sienna. What attentions everyone paid to Brother Body! And one day a companion whispered in my ear, It is Brother Elias.

Brother Francis.

And Brother Elias have you come all the way from Assisi?

I have, Brother Francis.

And what brings you so far, brother?

I received word that you were ill.

Ah brother I have been ill a long while now. And what else did you hear?

There was silence a moment.

That both Sienna and Perugia lay claim to your body.

I feared I would choke with the laughter.

My *body?*

This body?

You must be joking with me, brother. Poor little Brother Body?

This is no laughing matter, Brother Francis. They threaten one another to gain it once you are dead, each claiming it as their due.

And well they would have to contend for it. I fear they will find there is hardly enough left to be in one place let alone in two.

Again silence. It always worried me how little Brother Elias laughed. I took a deep breath.

Well brother I know it is your job as head of the order to look after us all. But I think none of us can have any use for what will be left after Sister Bodily Death has given me the kiss of peace.

Well never mind the reasons Brother Elias then gave to carry me back to Assisi. Brother Elias wanted it. The rule and life of the Least Brothers is to live in obedience as it is to live in chastity and with nothing of their own and to follow the teaching and the footprints of our Lord Jesus Christ. But for my part, I simply desired to be back at the Little Portion.

The new cloak Brother Elias gave me to wear weighed heavily on me. I had not touched cloth such as it was made of in twenty years. I asked him to free me from it.

How would it look to others, Brother Francis, to see you in nothing but this sackcloth? Even the patches have patches!

Ah but Brother Elias, please. How will it look to others to see me in the clothing of a rich man?

I think no one will mistake you.

See for yourself, brother, I said. I have a tunic and I have a cord and drawers. Please let that be all, I asked. It is enough.

It is not enough, he said.

I will obey you, I answered. But to my soul and to my God I said again, It is enough.

We traveled as far as Celle near Cortona and Brother Elias declared we would stop there to rest awhile. While at the place of the brothers I grew worse and could take no food and little Brother Body swelled up as if afraid to be dwindling to nothing. Then I asked Brother Elias to take me on to Assisi and he agreed on condition we wait for Assisi to send soldiers to guard our journey. And so we waited.

And one day a poor man came to the place weeping because his wife had just died. His family was hungry, he said. And I heard Elias tell him, We ourselves have taken a vow of poverty. Here is bread. But we have nothing more to give you.

Because this was not the kind of bread that would satisfy this poor man's hunger he soon went on his way.

As he passed my doorway I called out to him, God give you peace, brother!

Peace be with you, he said.

What alms did the brothers give you, son?

They had nothing but a little bread to give me and my children, father.

Then I have something to give you. Here. I give you this cloak on condition that you part with it to no one unless he buys it from you. And look, son—feel what soft new wool it is. So be sure to get a good price for it. Yes?

Yes, father.

When he left I called, Brother Leo, are you near?

Here I am, father. Are you well?

By the grace of God I am very well, Brother Leo. Hurry and tell Brother Elias with the other brothers that I have given away my cloak as an alms to the poor man who just now visited us.

I waited only a little before I heard fast footfalls and heard Let go! Let go! and No! and No! and It was a gift! Leo told me later that the good man held on with both hands. And praise the Creator of all persons, he was a big man and had strong hands. And I heard him say the condition I had given him and I heard the brothers conferring and Elias's voice and then steps coming and going and voices again and then again it was quiet.

Brother Elias came to the cell where I was.

Brother Francis, he said. You want to own nothing. I give you nothing to own, brother. This cloak is mine. I have just bought it. I have just bought it for the second time. I want you to use this cloak. But this cloak— Do you understand me, brother? This cloak is not yours. You cannot give away what is not yours to give. You must agree that is fair.

That is fair, brother, I said.

He laid the cloak on the bed and went away. Brother Leo came to me. What price did it bring the man? I asked and Leo told me. A good price, I said. But it is a very good cloak, is it not, Brother Lamb?

✠

The knights sent by the people of Assisi carried me back to the city. They did not carry me to the Little Portion. They carried me to the bishop's palace where I stayed for some time although perhaps not for as long as it then seemed.

We arrived midsummer when the air is full of dragonflies and bees. The grasses smelled sweet in the sun. A few field poppies still bloomed orange and red. There was a little window in the room where they laid me and through it the light and the air could minister to me.

And I had many visitors at the bishop's palace. One day an old friend, a doctor from Arezzo, John Buono, came to visit. John spoke to Brother Leo for a long while and then he pushed and patted and poked about at what remained of Brother Body. And then he took my hand and for a time we stayed together quietly. When he seemed to feel a little better I asked, And so what do you think about this dropsical disease of mine?

Dearest brother, he said. All will be well.

That is certain, I agreed. But now tell me the truth. What do you make of this? And don't be afraid to tell me. Our good God has given me such grace that I am, believe me, as happy to live as I am to die.

According to what we know of medicine, he said, your disease is incurable and you will die either at the end of September or perhaps early in October.

Now I had felt certain that our God had given me enough courage to face any diagnosis no matter how difficult but when I heard this I was so glad to be spared and could not pretend that I did not embrace this good news. And the relief and joy that rushed through me raised my hands and made me cry out, Welcome, dear Sister Death!

When I came to myself I said, If it is my Lord's pleasure that I should die soon, call Brother Angelo and Brother Leo and let them sing to me the song of Praise of God and of all God's creatures and of—I have another verse I want to add—especially of Sister Death and—

And just as fresh joy and the promise of rest had washed over me, now brothers and more brothers and others flooded into where I was laid. And the noise seemed like I was back in the battle of Perugia so many years earlier. Faces and faces close by mine and farther faces in shadows and faces in the light from candles held high by men from the bishop's household. Many faces and many voices and among them none that were Leo's or Angelo's. There were so many voices but none of them sang and none of them praised their God who made them and made all the other creatures. Praises of the Creatures! There was so much noise I no longer could even remember the tune.

I closed my eyes and tried to close my ears and other senses and felt from a long way off my hands raised and held and kissed, and my feet an even longer way off. I heard the faint clank-clank clank-clank of a censer and smelt the sharp sweet incense. I tried and tried to remember the words and the music but I could not and then I must have dozed.

When I opened my eyes again the air swirled all around me and dimly I could just make out a round white surface that seemed to gleam through the cloud. I said, Praised be You, my Lord, through Sister Moon.

But it was not Sister Moon but Brother Philip who dropped my left hand and fell back on his rump.

Forgive me, son, I whispered. I mistook you for another.

And the cloud seemed to grow thicker around me and around all and the candles flickered and I closed my eyes again, yearning to rest.

Let us begin, brothers, I said. Let us begin . . .

I was all the more eager to be back at the Little Portion now and so the brothers made a litter to carry me down the hill to the plain. Halfway there we stopped at the hospice of San Salvatore dei Crociferi. I asked the brothers carrying me to set the litter on the ground so that Assisi was before me. And I was able to raise myself just a little to say a blessing over that sweet city I would see no more. They carried me finally to the Little Portion and I knew I would not have to leave it again.

Having received such consolation it only remained for me to console those I was leaving.

Brother Rufino came and knelt beside where I lay and I asked, How is the Lady Clare and how are her ladies, brother?

She is very ill, mother. She cried very bitterly and said she was afraid she would not live to see you again.

Ah Clare.

And I wrote to her what I hoped would comfort her. I wrote the best words I knew.

Go and bring this letter to Lady Clare, I told the brother. It is all the presence I am able to give her.

And I prayed for her consolation.

And the brothers also, after one night when I brought up blood until morning, cried many tears. And I called all the brothers in the house to me and laid my hand on the head of each in turn and blessed him. Bring us bread, I said. Then I blessed the loaves and went to break them but did not have enough strength in my hands and so Brother Bernard broke the loaves and I handed a piece to each brother there. Eat all of it, I said. And we ate together.

Then there yet remained only our brother Lady Jacoba. The next morning I asked Leo to call the brothers to me. Write a letter to the Lady Jacoba of Settesoli, I said. You know how faithful and devoted she had been to us Least Brothers. Tell her of my condition and ask her to hurry to me with some plain ash-colored cloth and with it some of the marzipan she has often made for me in the city.

Suddenly we heard at the door the sound of many men and horses and there was a loud knocking.

Who will deliver the letter? Brother Angelo asked.

I asked, But who is at the door, brother?

Brother Lucidas came running in. What shall we do, father? The Lady Jacoba is here.

Of course she is.

Shall we allow her to enter and come to you?

Don't be silly, brother. Open the door and bring our brother Lady Jacoba in to see us.

And she came in having traveled from Rome with her children and her servants and she had brought with her what I had asked for in the letter and also what I had forgotten to ask for. And I was very glad to see her.

We spoke together and I felt stronger. So then Brother Jacoba ordered most of her company to leave, saying she would stay on with her children and a few attendants.

No, I told her. Because I myself will leave tomorrow and then you can leave with your whole company the day after.

I was unable to eat but she put a little of the marzipan on my tongue. I told her, It is as delicious as I remembered and hoped.

Near twilight the next day I woke and knew that my time had nearly come. Many larks flew about outside the Little Portion for a long time and with much singing and calling. I had always thought that if I could talk to the Emperor I would beg him for the love of God to grant my prayer and to publish an edict forbidding anyone to trap our sisters the larks or to do them any harm. And every year at Christmas everyone would be obliged to throw grain on the roads outside cities and towns so that on this day the birds and especially our sisters the larks would be able to feast.

I sang the Praises one more time but the verse about Brother Fire I sang twice. It was always my favorite part.

I am brought to my last moments, brothers, I told those who waited with me. Take off my tunic now and lay me naked on the naked ground.

And the brothers did so.

Dear brothers, I said. I have done what was mine to do. May Christ teach you what you are to do.

Then my heart was glad indeed because I kept faith with Lady Poverty to the end and died in her arms.

Francis's Last Will for Clare

I, little Brother Francis, want to follow the life and poverty of our most high Lord Jesus Christ and his most holy mother and to persevere in this to the end and I ask and counsel you, Ladies, to live always in this most holy life and in poverty. And keep most careful watch that you never depart from this through the teaching or advice of anyone.

The Canticle of the Sun
linoleum block print
16" × 12"

· 7 ·

A S MUST BE TRUE FOR EACH OF US, my death was my life's master-work, yes, but the song I wrote of the creatures I think comes near to it. How gracious God is to give us songs. And God gave me a life bursting with songs. Especially when I would be traveling along a road or walking through mead-ows or woods I would so often hear God murmuring to me of love. The rivers, the nightingales and doves and larks, the wind in the oaks and in the olive leaves, the burning fire sing of love. The little lambs' bleating in the springtime is a glorious song! Ah lambs— A miracle! Each one! And those with no voice sing without voice. They themselves are words and tune. The rocks and the hills sing by their being and the flowers by their sweetness.

And surely even Brother Worm praises God by his lowliness. That is why I would pick up a worm from the road when I found him and put him in a safe place where he would not be stepped on by people passing by. All that have been created serve their

Creator by being what they are. And all praise the God who loves them immeasurably and who is immeasurably lovable to all that has been made.

Sometimes the gifts and the goodness overwhelmed me—I was so in love—say rather I felt myself the one with whom God so utterly was in love— Sometimes I became drunk with it! The brothers laughed to see me forget where I was going and picking up a stick from the ground set it to my shoulder as a fiddle with another stick for a bow and sing for sheer abundance of joy. Sometimes God gave me the words and tunes and I sang them as a child hands back to his mother some small part of what his mother has just a moment before given him. Often my love songs to the lovely One were those the troubadours taught me.

> Can l'erba fresch'e.lh folha par,
> E la flors boton'el verjan,
> E.l rossinhols autet e clar
> Leva sa votz e mou so chan,
> Joi ai de lui e joi ai de la flor,
> E joi de me e de midons major—
> Daus totas partz sui de joi claus e sens,
> Mas sel es jois que totz autres jois vens.

> Ai las, com mor de cossirar.
> Que manhatz vetz en cossir tan,
> Lairo m'en poirian portar
> Que re no sabria que.s fan.
> Per Deu, Amors, be.m trobas vensedor,
> Ab paucs d'amics e ses autre senhor.

Car una vetz tan midons no destrens
Abans qu'eu fos del dezirer estens?

Brother Leo who was often with me knew no French. And now you must translate for me, he would say after I returned to my senses. I was glad when Brother Pacificus was with us because less of the music faded when he would translate. But when it was just Leo together with me then I would translate as best I could. Sometimes I needed him to help me remember what song I had sung.

Can l'erba fresch'e.lh, he would remind me.

When the fresh grass and leaf appear and the flower blossoms on the bough—and the nightingale raises high and clear its voice and pours out its song—I take joy in it—and joy for the flower—and for myself and my lady even more. On all sides I am surrounded by joy—but this is a joy overwhelming all others.

It is beautiful, father. Go on.

Alas how I die of deep thought. Often I am so deep in thought that thieves could carry me off and I'd know nothing of it. By God, Love, you find me easy to conquer with few friends—

I am your friend, father.

My son, you are a good gift of our good God.

Few friends. . . . By God, Love, you find me easy to conquer with few friends and no other lord. Why did you not once restrain my lady before I was consumed with desire?

Most of the songs that I made up were quite small just as I myself was small. But the song of Brother Sun, the Praises of the Creatures, was perhaps not so small. And this is how the song came about.

In the year before my death after I had come down from the mountain and had again lived with lepers, I then for a time traveled again to many villages and cities to proclaim the good news of the kingdom of God. But Brother Body grew more and more reluctant to do the work we had to do. For a long time Brother Body had complained of his liver his spleen his stomach and what not and now he complained of them all together and complained more often and more loudly. Yet it was not those parts but the disease of the eyes which brought Brother Body to his end. In those last years there were many times when I could see only dimly and tears ran down my face as if I wept. And the Lord Hugo bishop of Ostia could not bear the sight.

Brother, he said, it is not good to refuse to have your eyes treated, for your health and your life are very useful both to yourself and to others. You who have always sympathized with the ills of your brothers should not have such cruelty toward yourself, for this sickness is serious and you are in great and evident need. That is why I command you to submit to treatment.

Think of it this way, brother, he said. The doctor with God's help will make your pain go away so that you can again devote yourself to prayer.

Pain, I said. Pain too is prayer.

And Brother Elias likewise ordered me to be treated. I want to be there, he told me, when the doctor begins the treatment so that I can see to it that you receive the proper care and so that I can comfort you.

I humbly thanked him.

And so we set out for Rieti. And when we stopped to spend the night near San Damiano, Brother Body insisted on staying and would go no farther for a time. And in those sixty days I could bear no light from my lord Brother Sun or even from the smallest Brother Fire and so I stayed in the cell's darkness. And I could hear the wind in the olive grove and smell the wind and the straw and the soil but could see nothing except what the Lord showed me in dreams. I rested little in that time because of Brother Body's clamorings and the dreams I had were those of sleeplessness rather than of sleep.

In that little place of mats a great many little mice were living and the way in which they felt called to praise the Creator of us all was to scurry here and there. Their little footsteps rushing up then down then up then back distracted me when I tried to pray and woke me when I tried to sleep. And one night when the brothers had all gone to sleep and Brother Body nagged very loudly and the little mice scurried very quickly, around and around and around, my heart cried out for help to the One who made heaven and earth and every mouse in the earth.

And the voice of God answered my heart saying, Brother.

Here I am, I said.

There was silence.

Dear God, I said.

Silence.

These mice you have made.

Rejoice, God said.

My God my God how I long for you to bring me into your kingdom.

You will share my kingdom, Brother Francis. Wait patiently. All that I have will be yours. And is yours now. I made you. I am with you. Peace, brother—you are already sharing my kingdom.

Here is some porridge, father, Brother Leo's voice woke me in the morning. His hands lifted me to sit up.

I want to compose a new Song of Praises of the Lord for his creatures, Brother Leo.

I like the old one, father.

Ah little Brother Lamb, our God is praised and thanked by all the creatures and through all the creatures and on account of all the creatures and for all the creatures— What is it, brother?

One of the created mice ran up my habit, father.

I know you would never hurt him, brother. He praises his Maker.

I have him by the tail, father. May I not invite him to praise his Maker outside?

Certainly, brother. But the song. We enjoy the creatures every day and every night and cannot live without them and they serve us faithfully and yet through them the human race greatly offends our Creator. And every day we are ungrateful for our Creator's many graces and blessings and fail to praise as we should the giver of all these gifts. What if we had no sun for day no moon no stars no fire for night. We are all like blind men, brother, and it is God who gives us light to see. I felt Leo's hands take mine.

Your porridge, father.

Perhaps later, brother. Let me think a moment.

And I sat still and waited but no words came and no music.

And I continued to wait. All that day and all the next night no words no music came and I waited.

And then the Lord gave me a dream.

This is the dream.

I am sitting beside a river. I watch the water flowing darkly along and hear her jumping over the rocks as she journeys on. It has rained recently and I can smell the dampness in the earth and smell the trees' perfume. The sky is clear but clouding over in the west and the wind blows out of the northeast and brings me the smell of the Marches of Ancona and the sea beyond. I can even smell the hot dry lands beyond the sea. A great burning sun drops below a small rise and through the trees and between the clouds I can see it light up the sky with the colors of flames. And then suddenly I realize that the sky not only burns with colors, the sky is on fire, and I am afraid. Is this the end of the world? I can see the sparks pierce the air and hear the crackling but then I look down and see dear Brother Fire. Someone has built a small fire to kindly warm me and his burning is a merry song that he invites me to sing with him. I know the words to the song but cannot remember them. His sweet smoke caresses me as I watch the little flames dance and hear them sing. I look up and see past the trees my sister the moon risen full and clear. There is something that I am holding in my lap. I feel its weight and its shape and hold out my hands so that I can look at it and I can see clearly in the darkness that it is a skull, a human skull, it is my skull—though it never occurs to me in the dream to doubt that my head is still on my shoulders. I gaze at the skull and think how beautiful the firelight behind it is, almost like a living crown, and I watch the light, flickering and steady, touch my hands and wrists and cast little pools of brilliance onto the water as it runs by. And my heart burns within me. And then I woke.

A glyph/ornament appears centered at the top of the page.

And I opened my lips and heard, Most High, all-powerful, good Lord.

Then, Yours are the praises, the glory, the honor, and all blessing.

The words came first and then the melody and I taught it to the brothers that day. And Brother Leo needed no translation.

Most High, all-powerful, good Lord,
Yours are the praises, the glory, the honor, and all blessing.

To You alone, Most High, do they belong,
and no one is worthy to mention Your name.

Praised be You, my Lord, with all your creatures,
especially Sir Brother Sun,

Who is the day and through whom You give us light.
And he is beautiful and radiant with great splendor,
and bears a likeness of You, Most High One.

Praised be You, my Lord, through Sister Moon and the
	stars,
in heaven You formed them clear and precious and
	beautiful.

Praised be You, my Lord, through Brother Wind,
and through the air, cloudy and serene, and every kind of
	weather
through which You give sustenance to Your creatures.

Praised be You, my Lord, through Sister Water,
who is very useful and humble and precious and chaste.

Praised be You, my Lord, through Brother Fire
through whom You light the night
and he is beautiful and playful and robust and strong.

Praised be you, my Lord, through our Sister Mother Earth,
who sustains and governs us,
and who produces varied fruits with colored flowers and
    herbs.

Praise and bless my Lord and give Him thanks
and serve Him with great humility.

And when the brothers sang it back to me my soul was filled
with sweetness and I said, Brothers, here is what I want us to do.

Brother Pacificus, you were the choirmaster at a noble court
where they called you the King of Verse before you left everything
to follow Christ on the road with Lady Poverty. Now the Lord has
given you a new song. Take it and take some of the other Least
Brothers and go through the whole world. I want the brother who
is best at preaching to speak to the people first and afterwards all
of you sing the Praises together as troubadours of God. And when
the Praises end one of you shall say to the listeners, Dear people,
we are God's troubadours and ask you to repay us for our song by
truly turning to God.

Because what are God's servants, my brothers, but God's troubadours who must breathe into the hearts of all persons and stir
them to spiritual joy?

The next day after the brothers had sung with me a while, Brother Giles came in and said, There is news from town, Brother Francis.

What news, brother?

You know of the feud between the bishop and the mayor—

We know, said Brother Morico, of the feud between the bishop and half of Assisi.

Those are the half he does not own, Brother Sylvester said.

Say rather those are the half whose homes or livelihoods are owned by him.

Go on, brother, said Rufino. Is it another lawsuit?

Not another lawsuit but this—now Bishop Guido has excommunicated the mayor. In return the mayor had trumpets sounded in the streets of the city and announced that every Assisan was forbidden to buy from or sell anything whatsoever to the bishop or to transact any business with him.

They spoke on but I no longer listened. Brothers, I said, please. It brings great disgrace on us when the bishop and mayor hate one another in this way and no one can make peace between them.

Brother Leo.

Father.

Go and find the mayor and tell him for me to go to the bishop's palace along with Assisi's most notable folk and everyone he can assemble.

Brothers Pacificus, Angelo, Rufino, Masseo.

Father.

Go and in the presence of the bishop of the mayor and of the entire gathering sing the Praises. But first let me teach you two new verses.

Praised be You, my Lord, through those who give pardon for
Your love
and bear infirmity and tribulation.

Blessed are those who endure in peace
for by You, Most High, they shall be crowned.

Be sure to put them after the herbs and fruits and flowers just
before the last verse.

Go, children. I have confidence that the Lord will put humility
and peace in their hearts and that they will return to their for-
mer friendship.

And then I prayed to the God who brings us peace.

Leo returned before the others and out of breath from running
told me.

Father. Father.

Son.

They wept and embraced one another.

Of course they did, Brother Leo. Now catch your breath. And
then tell me—Did you like the new verses?

It still remained for me to journey to Rieti because of the disease
of my eyes and because of Brother Elias. It was early autumn when
we traveled south along the road that skirts the hills and when
finally we reached the city Brother Elias told me, The bishop is
expecting us, Brother Francis, and will make us welcome at his
palace.

And my heart sank for fear that I would find great comforts and little consolation there. And so it was. And so I spoke to Brother Elias.

I beg you, brother, let me stay at the hermitage of the brothers of Fonte Colombo while I undergo the treatment for my eyes.

And he granted that Masseo and Leo might carry me up that steep hillside.

My heart lifted as we wound upwards through oak woods with holly all around and we were embraced by the silence I remembered from when I had stayed here on the journey from Rome two years earlier. I longed for the embrace of that silence.

The doctor came and with him came his salves and his plasters and his knives to open veins and his bandages to close them but my eyes grew only worse. And the day came when the doctor brought out his iron and set it in the fire.

I have no treatment left, the doctor told Brother Elias as they stood near me, but the most drastic of cauteries. See here, he said, we must cauterize all these veins from here—and I felt his fingertip trace from my jaw to my right eyebrow—to here.

Brother Leo, I whispered, you will break all the bones in my hand in a moment.

Oh father father father, he said, and I could feel his hand trembling and his body shake with crying.

Hush, hush, I told him. All will be well.

Please continue, I invited the doctor. But I feared that I lacked resolve and so spoke to the fire and said, Brother Fire, the Lord created you noble and useful among all the creatures. Be courteous to me in this hour for I have always loved you and will always love you for love of the Lord who created you. I pray our Creator who made us to temper your heat so that I can bear it.

And I blessed the fire with the sign of the cross and again invited the doctor to continue.

When later the brothers returned to where I was, I said, Fainthearts! So little faith! Why did you run away? I tell you the truth, I felt no pain at all, not even any heat from the fire.

Here, doctor, I said. If it is not burnt enough then start all over and burn the left side too!

I stayed with the brothers at Fonte Colombo for a time longer. We spent Christmas there of course. And the day of the Nativity, my favorite day of the whole year, fell on a Friday. And one of the brothers would not join the others in the feast.

Why will you not feast, Brother Morico? I asked.

Today is Friday, he said and his voice was long. We know, Brother Francis, do we not, that we must fast on Friday. I will eat some of the vegetables for the sake of fellowship but I have vowed that no meat shall pass my lips.

It is the day the Lamb of God came into the world, brother.

It is Friday so it is a fast.

You sin, brother, I told him, calling the day on which the child was born to us a day of fast.

He drew himself back. How can you say that, Brother Francis? How can you possibly wish that the Least Brothers would eat meat on a Friday no matter where that Friday might fall?

I'll tell you, brother, I said. It is my wish that even the walls should eat meat on such a day and if the walls cannot eat meat they should be smeared with meat on the outside.

✳

We finally left Rieti to travel back to Assisi by way of Sienna. When I was staying at the bishop's palace in Assisi I very often invited the brothers to sing the Praises of the Creatures. Especially at night when the guards who kept watch on my account could hear, I asked for the song to be sung.

And after the visit by John Buono the fresh joy that filled me added to the song two more verses.

Praised be You, My Lord, through our Sister Bodily Death,
from whom no one living can escape.

Woe to those who die in mortal sin.
Blessed are those whom death will find in Your most holy will,
for the second death shall do them no harm.

And Brother Angelo and Brother Leo came and stood near me. Their voices seemed out of pitch but I set my mind not on the melody of the voice but on the harmony of the soul in harmony with God.

And the first time I heard the brothers sing it through from beginning to end I remembered the skull with the living crown of flame in the dream and I knew that the song was complete and I rejoiced greatly that soon my life as well would be complete.

And with Brother Body so clamorous in those days the Least Brothers would sing with me more often during the day and in the night. And I rejoiced and was comforted.

And one day Brother Elias came to where I was and stood near my head and said, My dearest brother, I am very consoled and edified to see your joy in such affliction and sickness. But the people of this city venerate you as a saint and all are well aware that you will soon die of your incurable disease. So when they hear this singing from morning to night and all throughout the night, they might think to themselves, How can this man show so much joy when he is about to die? Should he not be preparing himself for death?

I tried to sit up but could not. Believe me, brother, I said, I think of death as I have often thought of death, day and night.

I was able to come up on one elbow and out of breath with that effort said, Brother. Let me rejoice in the Lord and sing his praises in the midst of my infirmities. It is by God's mercy that I can rejoice in the most-high and only good God.

And by the mercy of God, Brother Elias left me alone and soon I was able to travel back to the Little Portion to meet Sister Death. On that day as sunset drew near I sang the Praises until I could sing no longer. Brothers, I whispered, you would do me the greatest kindness to sing the Praises of the Lord. And please, dear ones, sing it loudly. And so my friends escorted me as a bride going out to meet her beloved lover. They sang

Most High, all-powerful, good Lord,
Yours are the praises, the glory, the honor, and all blessing.

To You alone, Most High, do they belong,
and no one is worthy to mention Your name.

Praised be You, my Lord, with all your creatures,
especially Sir Brother Sun,

Who is the day and through whom You give us light.
And he is beautiful and radiant with great splendor,
and bears a likeness of You, Most High One.

Praised be You, my Lord, through Sister Moon and the stars,
in heaven You formed them clear and precious and beautiful.

Praised be You, my Lord, through Brother Wind,
and through the air, cloudy and serene, and every kind of
    weather
through which You give sustenance to Your creatures.

Praised be You, my Lord, through Sister Water,
who is very useful and humble and precious and chaste.

Praised be You, my Lord, through Brother Fire
through whom You light the night
and he is beautiful and playful and robust and strong.

Praised be you, my Lord, through our Sister Mother Earth,
who sustains and governs us,
and who produces varied fruits with colored flowers and
    herbs.

Praised be You, my Lord, through those who give pardon for
Your love
and bear infirmity and tribulation.

Blessed are those who endure in peace
for by You, Most High, they shall be crowned.

Praised be You, My Lord, through our Sister Bodily Death,
from whom no one living can escape.

Woe to those who die in mortal sin.
Blessed are those whom death will find in Your most holy
    will,
for the second death shall do them no harm.

Praise and bless my Lord and give Him thanks
and serve Him with great humility.

And bless them they did sing loudly.

Francis's Letter to Brother Leo

Brother Leo, send your Brother Francis greetings and peace.

As a mother to her child, I speak to you, my son. In this one word, this one piece of advice, I want to sum up all that we said on our journey and, in case hereafter you still find it necessary to come to me for advice, I say this to you—In whatever way you think you will best please our Lord God and follow in his footsteps and in his poverty, take that way with God's blessing and my obedience. And if you find it necessary for your peace of soul or to find comfort and you want to come to me, Leo, then come.

Afterword

Francis himself wrote scarcely anything. *And I, Francis* is based on those small writings, on the earliest accounts of Francis's life, and on other historical writings, and is partly my invention. The text is a response to Kathleen Frugé-Brown's paintings. Where Francis's own writings are quoted between the novella's chapters, I have used the translations in *Francis and Clare: The Complete Works* (Paulist Press) and *St. Francis of Assisi, Writings and Early Biographies: English Omnibus of the Sources for the Life of St. Francis* (Franciscan Herald Press), in a few instances combining elements of different translations and making minor changes for the sake of clarity and consistency. I have tried to be faithful to the Francis who emerges for me from the morass of canonization and legend.

L.G.D.

The paintings of this series were begun after I returned from a year in Italy; they are my homage, not only to Francis, but to Giotto and Cimabue, whose frescoes inspired me to tackle the subject. The linoleum block prints were then created from the imagery of the paintings, and were printed on BFK Reeves with the assistance of Hilary Culhane and Josef Venker, O.S.J.

The painting and print *The Death of Francis (After Giotto)* are based on Giotto's painting of the same subject in the church of Santa Croce in Florence.

K.F.-B.

Lauren Glen Dunlap   *Kathleen Frugé-Brown*

Lauren Glen Dunlap is a Seattle writer and editor. Her fiction has been published by Glen Press and InterVarsity Press. Her book reviews have appeared in the *Women's Review of Books*, the *Seattle Times*, the *San Francisco Chronicle*, and *Belles Letters*. She spent three years researching the available sources on Francis.

Kathleen Frugé-Brown lives and paints in the Pacific Northwest. She has exhibited her work in Italy, Canada, and the United States. A year spent in Italy—in particular, her study of Giotto and Cimabue—laid the groundwork for the series of paintings on Francis's life.

Also published by Continuum

St Francis of Assisi
The Legend and the Life
Michael Robson

"This is one of the best of recent lives of St Francis: at once readable, learned, perceptive and reliable."

—*The Tablet*

"This is a deeply moving and interesting book, at once a compelling and thought-provoking read for all admirers of St Francis and a valuable contribution to Franciscan studies."

—*Priests and People*

Michael Robson, OFM, is the Dean and Fellow of Saint Edmund's College, Cambridge, and Senior Member of the Divinity Faculty.

Francis of Assisi
Chiara Frugoni

"A respectful, insightful biography of St. Francis. Rather than concentrating solely on the previously well documented life and times of the remarkable visionary and ascetic, the author attempts to delve into the psyche of St. Francis, analyzing his motivations and ambitions within the historical context of the late twelfth and early-thirteenth centuries. . . . Approaching her subject from a philosophical and social angle, Frugoni analyzes the nature and significance of Francis' mysticism, introspection, and interpersonal relationships. A thoughtful and provocative examination."

—*Booklist*

"A new biography of the great ecumenical saint of Christendom, written by the professor of medieval history at the University of Rome. A straight-forward style that can be read by young people as well as adults. A nice way to introduce St. Francis to someone who might not know him."

—*The Living Church*

Francis of Assisi's Canticle of the Creatures
A Modern Spiritual Path
Paul M. Allen and Joan deRis Allen

"A historically and intellectually fulfilling foray into the heart behind the work of this most loved of saints."

—*NAPRA Review*

"Not a biography of Saint Francis per se, this book is perhaps best read as a collection of fragments organized around a nature mysticism rooted in Franciscan spirituality. . . .Those who seek flashes of insight, including a Western mystical tradition that may help modern readers re-conceive the liberal arts, will be richly rewarded. An entirely appropriate way of encountering the humility of Francis at the heart of Franciscan spirituality."

—*Booklist*

The late Paul M. Allen and Joan deRis Allen are the co-authors of *Fingal's Cave, the Poems of Ossian, and Celtic Christianity.*